Poems of Christmas Delights

A Treasury of Christmas Poetry

Capturing the Magic of the Holidays in Verse

Olivia Rosewood Thompson

Copyright ©2023 Olivia Rosewood Thompson
All rights reserved.

No part of this book may be reproduced, stored in a retrieval system, or transmitted in any form or by any means, electronic, mechanical, photocopying, recording, or otherwise, without the prior written permission of the publisher, except for brief quotations used in reviews.

This book is a work of fiction. Names, characters, places, and incidents are either the product of the author's imagination or are used fictitiously. Any resemblance to actual persons, living or dead, events, or locales is entirely coincidental.

The views and opinions expressed in this book are solely those of the author and do not necessarily reflect the official policy or position of any organization or individual mentioned within.

The author has made every effort to ensure the accuracy of the information within this book was correct at time of publication. However, the author does not assume and hereby disclaims any liability to any party for any loss, damage, or disruption caused by errors or omissions, whether such errors or omissions result from negligence, accident, or any other cause.

A Celebration of Christmas Poems

Amidst the hushed wonder of snowfall and the cozy glow of twinkling lights, the spirit of Christmas weaves its timeless magic. In "Christmas Whispers: Poems of Yuletide Delights," I, Olivia Rosewood Thompson, invite you on a poetic journey through the heartwarming embrace of this cherished season.

This collection marks the culmination of a delightful journey through the four seasons, and what better way to conclude than with a celebration of winter's enchantment? Within the pages of this book, you'll find fifty verses brimming with the joys and wonders that define the holiday season.

Each poem is a tapestry of emotions, carefully crafted to evoke the warmth of family gatherings, the joy of giving, and the beauty of winter landscapes. From the sound of carolers' harmonies to the scent of freshly baked cookies, every cherished aspect of Christmas finds its voice in these verses.

As you immerse yourself in these poetic whispers, I hope you'll find comfort, inspiration, and a renewed appreciation for the simple pleasures that bring us together during this time of year. Share these poems with loved ones, and let the spirit of Christmas illuminate your hearts and homes.

May "Christmas Whispers: Poems of Yuletide Delights" be a treasured companion during the festive season, reminding you of the joyous traditions that bind us as a global community. From my heart to yours, I extend warmest wishes for a Merry Christmas filled with love, laughter, and the magic of the holiday season.

With love and gratitude,

Olivia Rosewood Thompson

"Auld Lang Syne, Anew"

In the midnight's embrace, we stand,
Hand in hand, a hopeful band,
With memories etched deep and true,
We bid the old year a fond adieu.

As stars adorn the skies above,
We welcome the dawn, with hearts of love,
In every verse, a fresh start we find,
Auld Lang Syne, anew in mind.

Through laughter shared and tears we shed,
In unity, our souls are wed,
With a toast to dreams yet to unfurl,
We embrace the new with joy and zeal.

The moments pass, swift and fleet,
But in our hearts, the memories keep,
So let us sing, let's raise our wine,
Auld Lang Syne, anew we'll shine.

"Whispers of Snowflakes"

Soft whispers of snowflakes, a waltz from the skies,
With each delicate descent, a moment of surprise,
They dance through the night in their frozen flight,
Covering the world in a blanket of white.

Their silent symphony, a magical display,
Creating a wonderland, where dreams can play,
As they twirl and flutter, with grace they abound,
In this wintry ballet, a beauty profound.

A hushed serenade, a tale they unfold,
Of secrets whispered, of stories untold,
They paint the earth with their icy art,
A masterpiece crafted from nature's heart.

In the stillness of winter, they softly land,
A touch of wonder from the Maker's hand,
Oh, the whispers of snowflakes, a marvel to see,
In their fleeting dance, they set the heart free.

"Candlelit Serenade"

In the glow of candlelight's tender flame,
A serenade unfolds, a cherished name,
With flickering dance, shadows entwine,
A symphony of love, yours and mine.

Soft melodies, like whispers they play,
As stars above, their blessings convey,
A serenade of hearts, forever entwined,
In the warm embrace of love defined.

With every note, emotions ignite,
A candlelit dance, a celestial flight,
The music weaves, a tapestry grand,
As two souls unite, hand in hand.

In this tender moment, forever we'll bide,
A candlelit serenade, love's sweet guide,
Through trials and triumphs, side by side,
With each passing day, our love amplified.

"Gingerbread Dreams"

In the warmth of the oven, a fragrance so sweet,
Gingerbread dreams come to life, a delight to meet,
With cinnamon swirls and sugar so fine,
A cookie-crafted world, where wonders align.

In a land of icing and candy delights,
Gingerbread houses, a magical sight,
With gumdrop roofs and windows aglow,
A fairytale scene, like the soft falling snow.

Tiny gingerbread people, so sugar-coated,
Their dreams take flight, hearts forever devoted,
Amidst frosting meadows, they laugh and they play,
In a sugary haven, where they dance all day.

Oh, the joy in each bite, the memories they hold,
Gingerbread dreams, a tale to be told,
From the warmth of the oven to our hearts they'll gleam,
Forever cherished, these sweet gingerbread dreams.

"Starlit Wonders"

Starlit wonders fill the sky,
A dazzling dance, so vast, so high,
In the night's embrace, they glow,
Guiding hearts where love may go.

Each twinkle whispers, "Believe and dream,"
In the magic of Christmas, love does gleam,
Beneath their light, we come together,
In this season, hearts tethered forever.

In starlit wonders, hope takes flight,
A beacon of joy, so pure and bright,
This holy night, a timeless tale,
Of love's embrace, we'll forever hail.

"Mistletoe Moments"

Beneath the mistletoe's embrace,
In this enchanted, hallowed space,
Two hearts drawn close, a dance they find,
In moments sweet, their souls entwined.

With cheeks a-blush and smiles that gleam,
Mistletoe moments, like a dream,
A tender kiss, a whispered vow,
Underneath its boughs, love does avow.

In the season's glow, love takes flight,
Mistletoe's magic, a wondrous sight,
In every touch, a promise made,
Of love that blossoms and will not fade.

As carolers sing and candles glow,
Mistletoe moments, they softly bestow,
A love that grows with each passing day,
In this Christmas enchantment, forever they'll stay.

"Frosty Fantasia"

In winter's grip, a world of white,
Frosty Fantasia comes to light,
A symphony of ice and snow,
Nature's art in a magical show.

With frosted fingers, trees extend,
A frozen dance, a wintry blend,
In sparkling mirth, the land does gleam,
A waltz of wonder, a frozen dream.

Each snowflake's touch, a brushstroke fine,
Paints a canvas, so divine,
Frosty Fantasia, a sight to behold,
In nature's masterpiece, stories unfold.

In this frozen realm, we're invited to play,
A snowy wonderland, we'll gladly stay,
With laughter and joy, our spirits ignite,
Frosty Fantasia, a delight in the night.

"Cherished Traditions"

Amidst winter's snowy hue,
Cherished traditions, old and true,
Gathered 'round the Christmas tree,
Love and joy, our hearts decree.

In twinkling lights that softly gleam,
Cherished traditions, like a dream,
Through laughter shared and hugs so tight,
We celebrate with pure delight.

From carolers' songs to cocoa's sip,
Cherished traditions, hearts equipped,
In every moment, love's embrace,
Christmas magic fills the space.

With grateful hearts and spirits bright,
Cherished traditions, love takes flight,
In this season of pure bliss,
A treasured time we'll never miss..

"Silver Bells' Lullaby"

In the hush of the winter night,
Silver bells gently take flight,
A lullaby they softly play,
As stars above join their ballet.

Their melody, a soothing balm,
In the stillness, a tranquil calm,
Through snow-kissed dreams, they guide,
A serenade, side by side.

In the city's glow, they chime,
Silver bells, a wondrous rhyme,
Their lullaby, a sweet refrain,
A lulling comfort to remain.

As snowflakes fall, a gentle hush,
Silver bells sing, in whispers lush,
In their lullaby, dreams ignite,
Underneath the starry night.

"Tinsel and Twinkles"

Tinsel and twinkles, a dazzling sight,
Adorning homes in the soft moonlight,
With shimmering grace, they decorate,
A magical spell, they create.

In every corner, a glow they bring,
Tinsel and twinkles, they softly sing,
A symphony of light and glee,
In this festive jubilee.

They dance on branches, bright and grand,
Tinsel and twinkles, hand in hand,
Their magic weaves a tapestry,
Of Christmas joy and harmony.

Through starlit nights and snowy days,
Tinsel and twinkles, in myriad ways,
Fill hearts with wonder, young and old,
In a world of glimmer and gold.

"Midnight's Blessing"

In the hush of midnight's grace,
A blessing falls upon this place,
When stars adorn the velvet skies,
A sacred hush, a lullaby.

The world at rest, in slumber's keep,
Midnight's blessing, gentle and deep,
With moonbeams' touch, a tender glow,
A moment cherished, hearts bestow.

In dreams that weave and souls that soar,
Midnight's blessing, forevermore,
A whispered prayer, a hope aligned,
In the stillness of the mind.

As time stands still in this embrace,
Midnight's blessing, love's embrace,
A moment frozen, yet alive,
In midnight's blessing, we'll survive.

"Reindeer's Reverie"

Beneath the moon's soft silver gleam,
Reindeer's reverie, a wintry dream,
In the snowy night, they take flight,
Through the starry canvas, shining bright.

Their hooves prance on the icy ground,
Reindeer's reverie, a magical sound,
With bells that chime and spirits high,
In the northern sky, they dance and fly.

In Santa's sleigh, a grand delight,
Reindeer's reverie, a wondrous sight,
They journey forth, with hearts aglow,
Spreading joy wherever they go.

In the children's eyes, a spark ignites,
Reindeer's reverie, on Christmas nights,
Their boundless spirit, a guiding force,
In this season's love, they endorse.

"Sugarplum Fantasy"

In the land of dreams and sweets,
Sugarplum fantasy, where joy repeats,
Dancers twirl in sugar-spun attire,
In this magical realm, hearts aspire.

Candy canes that reach the skies,
Sugarplum fantasy, a sweet surprise,
Gumdrops glisten, enchanting scenes,
A world of wonder, in vibrant greens.

The Nutcracker leads the way,
Sugarplum fantasy, a grand display,
With every leap and graceful bend,
A dance of magic, they transcend.

In this reverie, we find delight,
Sugarplum fantasy, through the night,
A symphony of colors and delight,
In sugar-sparkled dreams so bright.

"Yuletide Embrace"

In the Yuletide's warm embrace,
Hearts connect in a sacred space,
Gathered 'round the hearth's embrace,
Love and joy, we interlace.

Through snow-kissed nights and twinkling lights,
Yuletide embrace, a cozy sight,
In laughter shared and carols sung,
A symphony of love, we're among.

With every hug and tender kiss,
Yuletide embrace, a cherished bliss,
In the spirit of giving, we unite,
A bond that glows, forever bright.

In this season's glow, love's the key,
Yuletide embrace, it sets us free,
To love, to share, to understand,
In this Yuletide's embrace, we'll stand.

"Evergreen Euphony"

Amidst the pines, a symphony,
Evergreen euphony, a melody,
The rustle of leaves in the breeze,
Nature's harmony, at ease.

With each swaying branch, a note,
Evergreen euphony, music afloat,
In the forest's hush, a soothing sound,
A serenade, pure and profound.

The whispers of trees, a gentle hum,
Evergreen euphony, a rhythmic strum,
In this tranquil world they dwell,
A song of peace they softly tell.

As snowflakes fall and silence grows,
Evergreen euphony, it overflows,
A timeless cadence in the air,
Nature's lullaby, so rare.

"Wreaths of Love"

In evergreen circles, they entwine,
Wreaths of love, a symbol divine,
With berries red and ribbons bright,
They speak of joy and love's delight.

With every bough and fragrant pine,
Wreaths of love, in homes they shine,
A welcome sight on doors so grand,
A gesture warm, hearts understand.

In winter's chill, their beauty weaves,
Wreaths of love, the heart retrieves,
A reminder true, in this season's art,
Of love that binds, never to depart.

"Cocoa's Caress"

In the chill of winter's air,
Cocoa's caress, a warmth so rare,
With each velvety sip we take,
A comforting hug, a dream to wake.

In cocoa's depths, flavors blend,
Cocoa's caress, a true friend,
In marshmallow clouds and chocolate bliss,
A moment of solace, a sweetened kiss.

As snowflakes fall and winds may blow,
Cocoa's caress, a cozy glow,
In every cup, memories trace,
A comforting embrace, a fond embrace.

So let us savor this delight,
Cocoa's caress, in the silent night,
With every sip, our spirits mend,
In cocoa's caress, love we'll send.

"Icy Elegance"

In winter's grasp, a sight serene,
Icy elegance, a frosty scene,
With crystal jewels, the world adorned,
A breathtaking view, nature's adorned.

In frozen lakes and snow-capped trees,
Icy elegance, the eye appease,
A delicate touch, a glistening sheen,
In winter's beauty, we're lost between.

The cold embrace, a chill so grand,
Icy elegance, across the land,
In every icicle that gleams,
A winter's wonder, it redeems.

"Sleigh Ride Sonnet"

Amidst the snow, a sleigh takes flight,
Sleigh ride sonnet, a winter's delight,
With bells that chime and runners glide,
In this snowy dance, hearts confide.

With horses' hooves in rhythmic beat,
Sleigh ride sonnet, a love's retreat,
In cozy blankets, side by side,
A winter's tale, we'll forever ride.

Through frosty trails and starlit skies,
Sleigh ride sonnet, our spirits rise,
In laughter shared and rosy cheeks,
A memory cherished, love bespeaks.

As snowflakes twirl and moonbeams gleam,
Sleigh ride sonnet, a timeless theme,
In this winter's symphony, we find,
A love that's pure and intertwined.

"Gifts of Grace"

In ribbons tied and packages adorned,
Gifts of grace, with love adorned,
In giving, we find joy's embrace,
A gesture kind, a smile on each face.

With thoughtfulness and hearts aligned,
Gifts of grace, their beauty shined,
A token of love, both big and small,
In the act of giving, we stand tall.

In the joy of sharing, spirits lift,
Gifts of grace, a heartfelt gift,
With every present, a story to tell,
Of love and care, we know so well.

In the season's glow, their magic gleams,
Gifts of grace, like cherished dreams,
A symbol of love's warm embrace,
In each precious moment, we'll trace.

"Starry Night Sonata"

Beneath the canopy of twinkling light,
Starry Night Sonata, a symphony of sight,
The stars above, in graceful dance,
Compose a melody, a cosmic romance.

With each gleaming star, a note does play,
Starry Night Sonata, in the Milky Way,
Their twinkling chorus, a heavenly refrain,
In this celestial ballad, we remain.

In the moon's soft glow, their beauty sings,
Starry Night Sonata, a song that clings,
To hearts that seek the tranquil sky,
A serenade that helps dreams fly.

In this celestial sonata, hearts unite,
Starry Night Sonata, love takes flight,
Through galaxies and timeless space,
In the starlit night, we find our place.

"Snowman's Melody"

In the winter's hush, a snowman stands,
Snowman's melody, crafted by hands,
With coal-black eyes and a carrot nose,
A frozen smile, a pose he chose.

In buttoned coats and scarves so grand,
Snowman's melody, in icy land,
With twigs for arms and a hat on head,
A cheerful friend, by children led.

In snowy fields where laughter rings,
Snowman's melody, a joy it brings,
With every snowflake gently kissed,
A winter's tale, forever missed.

As snowman's heart is made of snow,
Snowman's melody, it seems to know,
That in this moment, love is found,
In snowy landscapes, all around.

"Angel's Anthem"

In celestial realms where angels soar,
Angel's anthem, a song evermore,
With wings of light and hearts so pure,
They sing of love that will endure.

Their voices rise in harmonious flight,
Angel's anthem, a celestial light,
A melody that fills the air,
With hope and peace beyond compare.

In silver stars and moon's soft glow,
Angel's anthem, it seems to flow,
A soothing balm, a gentle sound,
In this divine symphony, love is found.

As night descends and hearts take flight,
Angel's anthem, a gift of insight,
In every whisper, every chord,
A message of love, from heaven's board.

"The Nutcracker's Tale"

The Nutcracker's tale, a wondrous sight,
With toys that dance and soldiers march,
In the enchanted world, their story arch.

Beneath the stars, a battle ensues,
The Nutcracker's tale, a fight to choose,
With bravery and courage they stand,
In the land of dreams, a hero's hand.

In the snowflakes' waltz, they whirl,
The Nutcracker's tale, a snowy swirl,
With Clara's heart, they gently twine,
A bond of love, forever divine.

In the kingdom of sweets, they dance,
The Nutcracker's tale, a joyful trance,
With Sugar Plum Fairy's guiding grace,
A spectacle of wonder takes its place.

As the night unfolds, the tale unwinds,
The Nutcracker's tale, a dream that binds,
In this cherished fable, love does bloom,
A timeless story, forever in bloom.

"Cozy Fireside Rhymes"

In a magical land where dreams take flight,
By the fireside's warm embrace,
Cozy fireside rhymes, we embrace,
With crackling logs and flickering light,
In this haven, hearts unite.

As winter's chill is held at bay,
Cozy fireside rhymes, we'll stay,
With mugs of cocoa, sweet and warm,
A place where love and laughter swarm.

In whispered tales and tender verse,
Cozy fireside rhymes immerse,
In each stanza, a tale is told,
Of memories cherished, pure as gold.

With family close and friends so dear,
Cozy fireside rhymes, they cheer,
In the comfort of this space,
We'll create memories to embrace.

"The Glow of Giving"

In the season's glow, hearts alight,
The glow of giving, a radiant sight,
With open hands and hearts that care,
A selfless act, love to share.

In gifts wrapped up with bows so neat,
The glow of giving, a love's heartbeat,
With each present, a piece of soul,
A gesture that makes the spirit whole.

In every smile and friendly gaze,
The glow of giving, a love's embrace,
A helping hand to lift one high,
In this season of love, we'll fly.

As kindness spreads from heart to heart,
The glow of giving, a work of art,
In every gesture, big or small,
A love that echoes, touching all.

"Jingle Bell Journey"

In winter's dance, a merry start,
Jingle Bell Journey, a joyous heart,
With each jingle, the bells resound,
A festive cheer, love does surround.

Through snowy paths and twinkling lights,
Jingle Bell Journey, in magical nights,
With laughter's echo and songs they play,
In this merry trek, we'll find our way.

In sleighs that glide through snow-kissed lands,
Jingle Bell Journey, in small bands,
With friends and family hand in hand,
We'll travel through this wonderland.

As bells ring out, their chimes so bright,
Jingle Bell Journey, a sweet delight,
In every step and joy we share,
A Christmas magic, beyond compare.

"Holly's Harmony"

In winter's embrace, a song takes flight,
Holly's harmony, a pure delight,
With leaves of green and berries red,
A symbol of love, forever spread.

In nature's chorus, they unite,
Holly's harmony, a joyous sight,
A melody in winter's chill,
A harmony that warms and stills.

With every branch and festive wreath,
Holly's harmony, a love beneath,
In this season's grace, they adorn,
A symbol of hope, from dusk till morn.

As carolers sing and hearts align,
Holly's harmony, a gift divine,
In every verse and every rhyme,
A Christmas spirit, so sublime..

"Magical Moonbeams"

Beneath the glow of the silver moon,
Magical moonbeams gently swoon,
In the night's embrace, they dance and play,
A mesmerizing sight, to light our way.

With each moonbeam's tender caress,
Magical moonbeams, a soft finesse,
They paint the world in hues so fair,
A dreamlike aura, in the midnight air.

In the stillness of the starry night,
Magical moonbeams, a tranquil sight,
They weave enchantment in the skies,
A celestial wonder that never dies.

As whispers of moonbeams softly sing,
Magical moonbeams, a gentle wing,
In this nocturnal serenade,
A moment of magic, forever laid.

"Winter's Waltz"

In winter's waltz, a graceful glide,
Winter's waltz, the snowflakes ride,
With each gentle step they take,
A dance of beauty, in snowflake's wake.

In icy swirls and frosty twirls,
Winter's waltz, the world unfurls,
A choreography of nature's art,
In this elegant dance, we're a part.

As moonlight casts a silver sheen,
Winter's waltz, a dreamlike scene,
With stars above, the night's ballet,
In this enchanting waltz, we sway.

Through frozen fields and snowy plains,
Winter's waltz, a cold refrain,
A symphony of winter's call,
In this snowy waltz, we enthrall.

"Heavenly Hymn"

In the hush of night's embrace,
Heavenly hymn, a sacred space,
With angel choirs, their voices blend,
A melody from realms transcendent.

Their harmonies in starlit skies,
Heavenly hymn, a sweet surprise,
A symphony of grace and love,
From realms above, they sing thereof.

In whispers soft and notes so clear,
Heavenly hymn, we long to hear,
A song that soothes the weary soul,
In this celestial chorus, we're whole.

As heaven's music gently sways,
Heavenly hymn, a serenade that stays,
In every heart, its echoes soar,
A heavenly hymn, forevermore.

"Gleaming Ornaments"

In shimmering hues, they hang with grace,
Gleaming ornaments, in their rightful place,
With silver and gold, they catch the light,
A dazzling display, both day and night.

From evergreen boughs, they gently sway,
Gleaming ornaments, in holiday array,
With memories old and stories untold,
A treasure trove of love they hold.

In twinkling lights, they dance and gleam,
Gleaming ornaments, like a festive dream,
Each one unique, a work of art,
A reflection of the soul and heart.

As snowflakes fall and carols sing,
Gleaming ornaments, their beauty they bring,
In this winter's glow, they enhance,
A season of joy and merry dance.

"Crimson Carols"

In the winter's night, a crimson hue,
Crimson carols, a melody so true,
With hearts ablaze and voices strong,
In this festive chorus, we belong.

In carols sung with love's embrace,
Crimson carols, a warm embrace,
A timeless tradition we revere,
In every verse, a message clear.

Through snowy streets and starlit skies,
Crimson carols, love's song does rise,
With every note, a tale we weave,
In this winter's eve, hearts believe.

As candles flicker, hearts entwine,
Crimson carols, a love's design,
In the harmony, we find delight,
A symphony of joy, in the night.

"Wonders of Winter"

In winter's wonder, a magical sight,
Wonders of winter, in soft moonlight,
With snowflakes falling from the sky,
A world transformed, as days go by.

In icy landscapes, nature's art,
Wonders of winter, they impart,
A beauty grand, both far and near,
In this snowy realm, we'll hold dear.

With frozen lakes and trees so bare,
Wonders of winter, everywhere,
In stillness found, a peaceful grace,
A tranquil scene, our hearts embrace.

As children play and laughter rings,
Wonders of winter, joy it brings,
In every moment, pure and bright,
A season's treasure, sheer delight.

"Peaceful Nightfall"

As the sun descends and shadows grow,
Peaceful nightfall, a tranquil glow,
With colors fading, stars appear,
In this gentle twilight, we hold dear.

In the stillness of the eventide,
Peaceful nightfall, hearts abide,
A moment of calm, a soothing balm,
In the moon's soft light, we find calm.

As the world slows down, day recedes,
Peaceful nightfall, a sense of peace,
With whispered prayers and silent dreams,
In this sacred time, love redeems.

In the quiet hours, hearts align,
Peaceful nightfall, a space to find,
A sanctuary in the twilight's call,
A moment of solace, for one and all.

"Sparkling Skies"

Beneath the vast expanse above,
Sparkling skies, a canvas of love,
With stars that twinkle, diamonds bright,
In this cosmic dance, hearts take flight.

In the moon's soft glow, dreams awake,
Sparkling skies, a shimmering lake,
With each glimmer, a wish is cast,
In this celestial beauty, time stands fast.

As constellations map their course,
Sparkling skies, a timeless force,
A story told, with ancient grace,
In every twinkle, a wondrous trace.

In the midnight's hush, they gleam,
Sparkling skies, a starlit theme,
In this grand spectacle, we're bound,
To mysteries above, we're crowned.

"Cascading Snowfall"

In winter's realm, a pure cascade,
Cascading snowfall, a serenade,
With flakes that dance from sky to ground,
A winter's tale, so soft, profound.

In every flake, a unique design,
Cascading snowfall, a gift divine,
With each descent, they gently call,
A blanket white, to cover all.

In nature's dance, they gracefully fall,
Cascading snowfall, enchanting all,
A symphony of peace and hush,
In this snowy dream, hearts do crush.

As snowflakes flutter and winds embrace,
Cascading snowfall, they interlace,
In this wintry scene, we find,
A wonderland, so pure, aligned.

"Deck the Halls"

With holly's green and mistletoe's kiss,
Deck the halls, a festive bliss,
In garlands hung and lights that shine,
A Christmas joy, so pure, divine.

With ornaments that gleam and glow,
Deck the halls, in yuletide show,
In every corner, a touch of cheer,
A celebration of the year.

In ribbons tied and wreaths adorned,
Deck the halls, in love adorned,
With family close and hearts aglow,
A merry gathering, we'll bestow.

As carolers sing and laughter rings,
Deck the halls, in caroling,
In this season's grand embrace,
A chorus of joy, takes its place.

"Enchanted Eve"

In the twilight's gleam, a magical hue,
Enchanted eve, a dream come true,
With stars that twinkle, the moon's soft light,
In this mystical moment, hearts take flight.

In the night's embrace, a wondrous spell,
Enchanted eve, where dreams dwell,
With whispers of wonder and mystery,
In this enchanted realm, we'll be.

As candles flicker and shadows dance,
Enchanted eve, a sweet romance,
In every corner, a touch of grace,
A magical aura, in this sacred space.

In this mystical hour, spirits rise,
Enchanted eve, where magic lies,
In each fleeting moment, a wish we believe,
A night of enchantment, this eve we receive.

"Golden Ribbons"

In glistening hues, a radiant sight,
Golden ribbons, a tapestry of light,
With every twist and graceful fold,
A touch of elegance they behold.

In gift-wrapped packages, they bind,
Golden ribbons, hearts entwined,
A symbol of love and sweet surprise,
In this golden glow, our spirits rise.

In festive splendor, they adorn,
Golden ribbons, in joy they're born,
With each bow tied, a moment shared,
A treasure wrapped, with love and care.

As they shimmer in the sun's embrace,
Golden ribbons, a warm embrace,
In this gilded dance, we'll find,
A touch of magic, so refined.

"Snowflake Sonata"

In winter's symphony, a gentle sound,
Snowflake Sonata, on frosty ground,
With flakes that twirl and softly play,
A sonata of snow, on a wintry day.

In delicate patterns, they design,
Snowflake Sonata, so pure, divine,
A dance of ice, in the chilly air,
A fleeting beauty, beyond compare.

Each snowflake's verse, a work of art,
Snowflake Sonata, from skies to heart,
With every fall, a tale they tell,
In this snowy sonata, we're under its spell.

As they drift and float in the breeze,
Snowflake Sonata, they gently appease,
In this winter's concerto, we'll abide,
A harmony of snowflakes, far and wide.

"Angel Wings and Halo Rings"

In the heavens above, a heavenly sight,
Angel wings and halo rings, a celestial light,
With grace they soar, in ethereal flight,
In this divine presence, all is right.

With wings of ivory and golden rings,
Angel wings and halo rings, joy it brings,
A chorus of angels, their voices unite,
In this celestial choir, love takes flight.

In their gentle embrace, hearts find peace,
Angel wings and halo rings, love's release,
A presence divine, a heavenly guide,
In this celestial realm, hearts reside.

As they watch over us, from realms above,
Angel wings and halo rings, pure love,
In their celestial dance, a seraphic rhyme,
A gift of grace, through the sands of time.

"Glowing Candles' Grace"

In the soft candlelight, a tranquil space,
Glowing candles' grace, a warm embrace,
With flickering flames that gently sway,
In their golden glow, worries allay.

In their radiant dance, shadows glide,
Glowing candles' grace, a calm inside,
A soothing balm for hearts that ache,
In this peaceful glow, solace we'll take.

As they illuminate the darkness deep,
Glowing candles' grace, love does seep,
In every corner, their light does bloom,
A tender glow that fills the room.

With their soft glow, spirits rise,
Glowing candles' grace, love replies,
In this warm ambience, we find,
A moment of peace, hearts intertwined.

"Midnight's Whispers"

In the stillness of the midnight hour,
Midnight's whispers, a gentle power,
With stars that twinkle in the dark,
In this mysterious hush, we embark.

In soft moonlight, secrets unfold,
Midnight's whispers, a tale retold,
A symphony of silence they create,
In this midnight serenade, we await.

As night owls hoot and crickets sing,
Midnight's whispers, a quiet wing,
In this magical moment, hearts converse,
A bond with the night, we immerse.

In the quietude, dreams take flight,
Midnight's whispers, a peaceful rite,
In this nocturnal realm, love finds,
A sacred space in midnight's binds.

"The Blessings of Bethlehem"

In the town of Bethlehem, so long ago,
The blessings of Bethlehem, a sacred glow,
With a humble birth in a stable bare,
A miracle of love, for all to share.

In the starlit sky, a guiding light,
The blessings of Bethlehem, shining bright,
A sign of hope for all mankind,
In this divine moment, grace we find.

With shepherds' awe and angels' song,
The blessings of Bethlehem, a love so strong,
A Savior born on that holy night,
A gift of salvation, in heavenly light.

In the manger's warmth, a newborn King,
The blessings of Bethlehem, they still ring,
A promise of peace and love's embrace,
In this timeless story, hearts find solace.

"Fireside Fables"

By the fireside's glow, a tale unfolds,
Fireside fables, of knights and trolls,
With every flicker of ember's light,
In these enchanting stories, we take flight.

In the storyteller's voice, magic weaves,
Fireside fables, in hearts it cleaves,
A world of wonder and dreams untold,
In these fireside fables, legends unfold.

With each character's journey, hearts entwine,
Fireside fables, in every line,
A tapestry of words, rich and deep,
In these wondrous tales, memories keep.

As shadows dance upon the wall,
Fireside fables, they enthrall,
In this cozy embrace, we find,
A moment of joy, of heart and mind.

"Frosted Window Panes"

Through frosted window panes, a scene,
Of winter's touch, so serene,
With delicate ice, a frosty lace,
In this winter's embrace, we'll find our place.

As snowflakes twirl and gently fall,
Frosted window panes, a snowy call,
A world transformed in shades of white,
In this winter wonderland, hearts take flight.

In the warmth inside, we stay,
Frosted window panes, in disarray,
With hearts aglow and laughter's ring,
A cozy haven, where memories sing.

As candlelight flickers and hearts align,
Frosted window panes, love does shine,
In this season's glow, a sense of peace,
A moment of joy, that'll never cease.

"Merry and Bright"

In the festive glow, hearts delight,
Merry and bright, a joyful sight,
With twinkling lights and colors gay,
In this merry season, love will sway.

In laughter's chorus and carols sung,
Merry and bright, bells are rung,
A celebration of love and cheer,
In this magical time of year.

With gifts exchanged and hugs so tight,
Merry and bright, love takes flight,
In each gesture, a touch of grace,
A smile that lights up every face.

As friends and family gather near,
Merry and bright, hearts endear,
In this merry company, we'll find,
A warmth that fills our souls, so kind.

"Celestial Delights"

In the celestial expanse above,
Celestial delights, a cosmic love,
With stars that shimmer in the night,
In this heavenly panorama, hearts take flight.

In galaxies vast and nebulas bright,
Celestial delights, a wondrous sight,
A dance of planets and moons that glide,
In this cosmic ballet, love does reside.

As comets streak across the sky,
Celestial delights, they catch the eye,
A celestial fireworks, grand display,
In this astral symphony, we'll sway.

With constellations, stories unfold,
Celestial delights, myths untold,
In every constellation's gleam,
A tapestry of dreams, it seems.

"Chorus of Joy"

In voices raised, a chorus of joy,
A symphony of love, nothing can destroy,
With hearts united, in harmonious glee,
In this jubilant chorus, we are free.

In laughter's echo and smiles so bright,
Chorus of joy, like stars in the night,
A melody of happiness, hearts entwine,
In this chorus of joy, love does shine.

With every note, a bond we form,
Chorus of joy, through any storm,
A song of hope that fills the air,
In this joyful chorus, we'll declare.

As hands are clasped and spirits lift,
Chorus of joy, a festive gift,
In this moment, love does mend,
A chorus of joy, that'll never end.

Copyright ©2023 Olivia Rosewood Thompson
All rights reserved.

No part of this book may be reproduced, stored in a retrieval system, or transmitted in any form or by any means, electronic, mechanical, photocopying, recording, or otherwise, without the prior written permission of the publisher, except for brief quotations used in reviews.

This book is a work of fiction. Names, characters, places, and incidents are either the product of the author's imagination or are used fictitiously. Any resemblance to actual persons, living or dead, events, or locales is entirely coincidental.

The views and opinions expressed in this book are solely those of the author and do not necessarily reflect the official policy or position of any organization or individual mentioned within.

The author has made every effort to ensure the accuracy of the information within this book was correct at time of publication. However, the author does not assume and hereby disclaims any liability to any party for any loss, damage, or disruption caused by errors or omissions, whether such errors or omissions result from negligence, accident, or any other cause.

Milton Keynes UK
Ingram Content Group UK Ltd.
UKHW020849240823
427393UK00006B/116